Ghost Maps

Ghost Maps
Poems for Carl Hruska

Erin Noteboom

Wolsak and Wynn . Toronto

Typeset in Palatino, printed in Canada by
The Coach House Printing Company, Toronto.

Front cover art: © Wendy Noteboom Ewell
Cover design: The Coach House Printing Company
Author's photograph: Patricia Bow
This collection won the CBC Canadian Literary Award in 2001 and was featured on CBC radio and in Air Canada's *enRoute* magazine. Individual poems have appeared in *The Malahat Review*, *PRISM international*, and *The New Quarterly*.

The publisher gratefully acknowledges support from the Canada Council for the Arts and the Ontario Arts Council for their support through a block grant.

The author expresses appreciation for support from the Canada Council for the Arts and the Ontario Arts Council through a Writers' Reserve grant and a grant from the Works in Progress Fund.

Wolsak and Wynn Publishers Ltd.
192 Spadina Avenue, Ste #315
Toronto, ON
Canada M5T 2C2

National Library of Canadian Cataloguing in Publication

Noteboom, Erin, 1972-
    Ghost Maps: poems for Carl Hruska / Erin Noteboom.

ISBN 0-919897-90-8

    I. Title.

PS8577.O7525G46 2003   C711',6   C2003-901956-X
PR9199.4.N66G46 2003

CONTENTS

EMPTY PAGE

THE STORY OF GHOST MAPS

THANKS

ACKNOWLEDGEMENTS

Carl Hruska

November 19, 1923 – January 5, 1997

drawn from visits
April – December 1996

GHOST MAPS

Off the ladder, he stumbles.
Puts his false foot down hard, and
all at once his leg
is there, he'd swear it — can feel
its hair stand up, bones open
to the blast
                    bones remember.
There is a theory
about this, the way pain builds its nest
like paper wasps
in a branch gone hollow.
The mind has maps, carries the ghost self
close and secret, like a man
buttoning a scalloped snapshot
into his heart's pocket.

FALL

LETTER HOME
    October 1944

He's heard that Kansas is a sea
of grass, but leaning on the transport's rail,
he does not see it. The dragonfly green
of wheat just up, or the baked-bread smell
of fields in August — nothing
like that. The Atlantic, all of it, is
as he imagined whales.
The grey backs blow and break,
roll down in deep dives. He was sick
eleven days.
                But a man can get used
to anything.
              Yesterday,
the first death. The cook's mate —
a Negro, first he's seen — who slipped and split
his lambswool head
on the hard mess table.
              The kind of thing
you don't live down, or wouldn't. They buried him
pretty plain, though out here
you couldn't call it burying.

TRAINING
Texas — August 1944

In his collarbone the rifle's kick
becomes an ache so deep
he does not feel it:

just a deafness in that ear,
a wisdom
            when the weather changes.

BROWN VELVET
Kansas – September 1943

Vivian wore brown velvet to my brother's wedding.
I liked it. Liked her in it.
                              When I came back,
she used to stroke my hair, say, soft, soft —
nights when I couldn't even shake.

THE HAND
Ardennes — November 1944

At first glance, he thinks:
            a glove
a white three-button dropped
in harrowed mud. It has
that length precisely.
There is no blood in it.

Come in, it says, its
            emptied gesture

FIRST

Ardennes – December 1944

Folks used to write me that
in letters: Got any Germans
yet? I was trying a while before
I knew for sure. I saw him fall
and later, forward, saw him
half-crawled from the hole.
Ever chop a black snake
with a hoe? It's hard
and easy.

SILENT NIGHT
Ardennes – Christmas 1944

At midnight the Angelus
falls soft into the foxholes.
Across the shattered field, someone
is singing
           Stille Nacht.

He takes aim at the sound.

The perfect trees
                lean in,
        listen.

WINTER

SHELTER
   Ardennes — January 1945

A church, once.

The roof above the altar
shelled in.

   Couldn't sleep.

Snow curls the angel's shoulders.

The monstrance opens
its round blank eye.

ICE

Ardennes — January 1945

They slept in stooks — standing,
leaning in like sheaves of wheat,
their wordless breath
a fog between them,
so that when they woke
their slung rifles were edged
with ice, their helmets
jack-frosted like store windows,
their tangled lashes sealed
as if with coins of silver.

LULLABY
    Ardennes — January 1945

you'll see wonderful things

catch step catch — frost
bite hobbles him two toes
black. In better times

you might go home
for this, though
    there'd be some shame

He walks — caught
in his head a snatch
of lullaby —

You'll see wonderful things
    his memory sings

    raisins and almonds

NIGHT
Ardennes — January 1945

The hardest thing
was night, all white
and the snow whipped up
in devils. Or worse,
still. That cold —
you could hear everything.
Trees that creak and crack
like rifles. Voices,
sometimes, words
you couldn't make out,
or cattle, bawling to be milked.

DREAMS

Ardennes — January 1945

In cold sleep his blood turned
to velvet. He woke and couldn't shake,
it was that thick.
                    Once he knocked
at a farmhouse where he hoped to steal
some socks. No one came
to the plain plank door.
But then, he meant nothing
by knocking, no more than a dog means,
who turns three times
into an ancient dream.

MORNING

You wouldn't believe how beautiful
it was. In the night the fog would freeze
and in the morning everything
was soft with it — ghosts of trees.
We advanced into open fields
the colour of apple blossom,
delicate with blue shadows.
Against that snow we stood out
like deer.
                    And then
the shelling would start.

VIVIAN KNITS
    Kansas — January 1945

Vivian knits at the kitchen window.
Snow like a strike of light
whitens one side of the windbreak,
and the light looks like snow
now that the squall has broken — thickened, clotted,
softly falling. The fields are blue.
A plume blows off the silo peak.
POWs are shovelling the roof
of the chicken coop, which is drifted
and sagging. Their faces shine
above their numbered jackets.
Their backs bend like pump handles.
She catches a snatch of laugh, a shout
that could be any language,
the flash of a boy's grin
as he sleds down on his shovel,
lands lightly, turns his back to pee.
Behind her, covered bread is rising
like a body. It's hard
to hate them. She's dropped a stitch.
She silences her needles
and pulls out her work.

WINTER WHITE
Ardennes — January 1945

Mid-afternoon in some nameless town
a door bangs, a woman comes running,
arms full of folded white. One sheet
flies out behind her like a banner, and
they understand. She's giving them linens,
winter camouflage. With no language,
he thanks her, and she presses to him,
weeping. When she runs he lifts
his hands and finds
a table cloth. Not lace,
but that stiff stuff,
cutwork. He cuts it
with his bayonet.
Pulls it over his head. Inside,
he smells the starch,
the ghost of iron.

NIGHT PATROL
Ardennes — January 1945

Snow sloughs from a pine bough —
you got to know the sound,
the kinds of crust: which would creak
and which would tick.
Got so you'd move
darn close to silence.

A LIGHT
Ardennes — January 1945

Once, on night patrol,
they came nose to nose
with German scouts.

Fog snaked through thick trees.
The moon shone
like a newsreel.
What was there
to say?

They exchange cigarettes
and silence. The moon
slips on. The stars take up
their fixed positions.

REST

Ardennes — January 1945

Cold enough to crack stone.
You couldn't lie down
in it — or even sit.

Even the springs of the rifles
slow.

NAMES (i)

Ardennes — February 1945

The new ones,
green, we lost so quick
sometimes I never learned them,
or learned two, you see,
like Smith and Jones, and never
straightened which was which.
Checked the tags, but it didn't fix
in my mind, which was which.

NAMES (ii)
Ardennes — February 1945

Gawosky took a slug
of secret brandy — *not a damn thing here*
has got my name on it — he spat,
jammed a bandage
to the blown tip of his ear.

It was a shell
that knew him. It called
and he opened his mouth
to answer.

A SCRATCH
Ardennes — February 1945

Not even worth a medal,
said the medic, wrapping up
a scarf of bandage. Just
a sneaky little something
that slipped the lace of his fingers
as he lay face down
in the foxhole — shrapnel
in the back of the neck. It bled,
but it was nothing, a scratch,
a scar to slick his fingers
when he turns his collar up against
some future evening: the window cracked
and the curtains stirring,
the hish of traffic
washing by.

THE GHOST
Ardennes — February 1945

He came down like a milkweed
for a kid to wish on: one paratrooper,
scattered by the wind.

You're supposed to wait
but no one did.

I saw
> *his teeth spin out*
like fireworks,
his bones fold
into the snow.
The chute
billowed
above him,
shimmered
and settled.

LETTER FROM VIVIAN
    Kansas — February 1945

No news, really.
It's been cold.
We lost a bull calf,
born too early.
Brought him to the kitchen,
but still, he shook himself out.
White star on his forehead.
A wet red coat.

DRAGON'S TEETH
German Border — February 1945

Vivian sends him boot liners,
so tight-knit he feels
the ache of her fingers
when he pulls them on.
He wants to write,
but what can he tell her —
the pillbox where concussion
left the untouched dead
bowed over hymnals.
They've made the Siegfried Line
and the papers are full
of victory. He kicks
through shattered concrete.
Gravel arcs and catches
in the churned earth,
white and grinning.

Spring

SPRING
Germany — March 1945

Against the yellow silk
of dawn, a blackbird
weaves her nest
of radar chaff
and human hair.

THE NEST

Germany — March 1945

Sully stumbled on this nest of bumblebees
and flapped like he was learning to fly.
He drew them right to me. God,
how we laughed, strafed
by that little army.

SWEETNESS
Germany — March 1945

The fire trickles away
and they inch forward.
Birds begin in the dark lace
of branches. A little wind
scatters red bud-casing.
He catches an ankle,
stumbles, slaps a hand
to a trunk and finds it
wet: a rivulet of sap running
from a bullet wound.
The thing that tripped him:
a gaping body. Looking down,
he sucks the sweetness
from his hungry fingers.

LIBERATION

Germany — March 1945

Cologne was the first place
we saw Germans.
Civilians, I mean.
The whole town twitched
like a curtain. A sniper
tumbled from a rooftop
turned out to be a tow-head kid
of maybe ten.
It was Sully who got him.
Can you imagine?

WOUND
Germany — March 1945

It wasn't the first,
but it was the first to go so deeply
into him —
through the shin,
between
those long fine bones,
their arch flying open —
a sudden eye —

Stupid, to get hit
so near the end.
There isn't any story to it,
if that's what you're hoping.

WASTE

It happened in an orchard.

Lying there, he stares
into the ragged holes that wasps have chewed
in windfall apples — soft
as mud, now, brown
as the hand of frost. Gone

to waste. By that alone
he might have guessed
at mines. This
    hungry country.

Black scissors swing
    from the medic's wrist.

White
    and pink-white
            the blossoms
tumble.

RITES

Germany — March 1945

A thumbnail's trace
across his forehead:
field medic marking dosage
with blue skin pencil.

For a moment,
it's all he can feel.

When they loosen his boot
he asks for blessing.

VISION
Germany — March 1945

Sully
dark heap dappled with petals —

Vivian, the morphine
is the colour of your hair —

THE STONE PICKERS
Kansas — March 1945

Vivian scrapes mud from the back stoop.
It's spring at last, the yard soft,
the new wheat vivid.
In the back field, men
are picking rock — the land's
first crop, and most faithful.

They pile stones in the boggy ditch.
Handsome feathers and bright shoulders
like dress uniforms, a pair of blackbirds
swings into the sky, crying and crying —

(polished shoes swing from the black car)

The stone pickers
are German, she knows, POWs.
Their seed, their harvest —

In her pocket, the telegram
has worn to softness
and begins to tear.

KINGDOMS
Army Hospital, France — March 1945

At the general hospital, they tidy things up:
officers in one room, grunts in others,
sorted out by wound. He figures
things could be worse: the gurney clicks by
the belly ward, the ward for guys
who caught it in the face.
The Kingdom of the Blind,
that's called. Though each room
is a kind of kingdom. At night,
in the Shu-mine ward, they line up
the shortened lumps of legs.

PURPLE HEART
Hospital Ship, English Channel — March 1945

The medal-pinners came to Dover
to meet the ship. I remember, we were supposed
to lie at attention. A man could die, and they'd only say
how fine his attention —

                              Never put my name
on anything, would you, Erin?

SILAGE

North Carolina — April 1945

At Fort Bragg, they teach him to change
his own dressing. He has a farmer's eye
for it, for silage — stuff cut green
and mulched for feed. Wet is bad,
and tight: the heat of rot can set
the stack on fire. He thinks of that
and twines his stump with gauze. How strange
it will be — the green prairie,
the prettiest time of year. When he left
they were burning the cornfields.
He smells again that yellow
smoulder, dreams
the sweep of horizon,
starlings rising,
home.

SUMMER

HOMECOMING
Omaha, Nebraska — April 1945

For nine months,
Vivian watched the eyes
of neighbours' houses.

Saw the service stars swing
on small red banners.

Saw the slow draw of blinds
in the broad grey weather.

Now the train judders
under Union Station.
The boiler huffs and shushes
and a machine
begins to speak.
She waits
to see the damage.

THE MIRROR

Troop train, Illinois — April 1945

Like a steam plume his thought hangs
over fields of new corn,
ditches ragged with pigweed
and rose, poplar windbreaks
where one might place
a fixed position.
The train's slow heartbeat has him half-asleep
when they pull past a station.
Against the sudden wall
the window silvers. Inches away,
the flash of his face.

NEWS

Kansas — July 1945

Vivian dashes in from thunder,
newspaper soaring over her head.
She stands in the kitchen, dripping,
laughing. She kisses me.
Her fingers
                  are inky,
her face printed
with news.

SNAPSHOT: WEDDING
        Kansas — July 1945

He's in uniform, all dark detail:
starched crease and pointed collar,
medals grey with colour.
She's in satin, more white
than clapboard, bright as glass,
as mirror. The wind lifts her hair
in a spray like water. She's twisting
to save her veil, laughing, lifting
a hand from which dark roses
tumble. He has not yet turned with her,
still looks through the camera.
Their shoes are dusty. His open mouth
a small dark seed.

WEDDING
Kansas — July 1945

A hot day, dusty. The boys still in
their velvet haircuts, the church all shut
and thick with broken colour. I remember
three men fainted.

Vivian wore satin.
The door behind her opened
and she shone there
like a parachute.

FLASH

She opens his clothes
with quick fingers, then
bends her head to the buckle
at his knee.

Her breath is hot.
Her bright hair sweeps his body.

He traces her ears,
noses the part of her hair,
then sees his leg
lying there,
on the crocheted top
of the dressing table,
like a practice rifle
waiting for oil.

HEAT LIGHTNING
Kansas — August 1945

Vivian knits a blanket in the creaking heat
of afternoon, the sun as flat as sheets
beyond plain, square windows.

How false
peace feels, sometimes, half a thing,
like heat lightning.

Sunset and the pluming chaff
is red and slow
as flares, falling,
falling. He remembers

bones are said
to knit:
            the silver flash
the click of needles.

THE DAY WE WON THE WAR
Kansas — August 1945

It was just after my wedding.
I was still learning to walk.
Round the side of the house,
Vivian puts out the laundry —
screech of pulley, then
the snick, snick of pins.
I hold to the drainpipe
and hoist rag and kerosene
to a nest of yellow jackets.
Orange slants through the oily smoke
and the sheets
                    snap.
When I went to war, it was simple
as handkerchiefs.

HOW MUCH OF THE MEMORY

CROSSING

Lost the farm with the leg and knew it
the first time he loaded hay.
Like a heavy sea, that heave,
that pitch. He lurched into the stooker,
sick. His stump bled.

How much of the memory
is carried in the body?
Lost bones speak to him of vision,
of deep water. Phantom,
it's called, that voice, that itch.

He took his GI bill,
got a degree: horticulture
fruit trees, mostly. Crossing apples,
he learned to open
gold rooms
of pollen.
            Petals fall,
heart-shaped, softer than leaves,
no less a loss.

NO HISTORY

The new house has no history —
no sleepless cellar where onions stir
in slatted bins, no big crab apple
to make its speech on wind.

From the window he turns,
creaking.

Vivian round and naked
in a square of moonlight.
He touches her belly:
scar-slick stretch marks
blooming like photographs
in a bath of silver.

THINNING THE BLOSSOM

His first orchard half
wild, haw trees toppling
snake fence, split heart wood,
unkempt apples rust-dappled knuckled
as an amputation.

In a row of cameo
and northern spy he eases the lopper
into crowns too thick
for light. Takes the base
of a scaffold branch, feels the beak
catch, resist, then
shear. The branch staggers loose,
swings from clasped twigs, tumbles.

All day, he does this
slow work. He has seen fire
do it quicker — shells popping limbs
with blind precision.
Through the twilight, now,
black dog bounding like a mortar.

WEARING THE SUN

His shirt comes off the line with heat
still in it, cut flecks of grass, pollen, dust
from the field they're tilling. He pulls it on while
Vivian folds the diapers: soft white squares
getting smaller, neat stacks for the drawer,
everything straight and clean except that he's wearing
all outdoors, and under that, a chill
that's tight as skin, delicate as buttons.

SETTING THE BEES

So early the sky still shows
its winter stars, as if night
were another season, Orion
laying down his sword,
his dogs stiff-legged, weary.
The bees sleep in his arms
as he bundles their slatted box
into the white ghosts of the orchard.
They won't stir till dawn,
pale sun pulling smoke
from frost. Against his chest
he rocks them, dreaming
their pollen-drenched darkness,
their sweet work when they wake
in a strange and haunted country.

TRACE

He stands at the door while snow
falls thick into the yard,
across the softened garden,
blackened vines and jumbled hills
of squash. Coatless, arms crossed,
he goes out to save the tricycle,
swings up the easy weight,
smells the faint tang of grease
and metal. In such still moments
the war fits its body's curves to his,
and time, like snow blossoming in water,
touches his face, vanishes.

GLARE

"Why do you suppose they do that,"
he says. He's looking at the soldiers,
bandannas tight around their heads,
and "Lampblack," he says and touches
the dust-soft cheekbones.
"Greasepaint." Liz snaps
the tuning knob. "For the glare."
Her hair swings between them.
"For the glare," he echoes.
His skin is blinding.
Liz smacks the side of the set
and the jungle flickers into snow.

GIVING AWAY

One daughter, then the other,
huddles against him in the close space
behind the side altar.

Giving away
Elizabeth, the youngest,
he feels for the first time in years that
phantom ocean, that inner door blowing open
into white light
and petals.
              What am I losing,
he wondered,
and kissed her cheek
for luck.

PICKING

Off the ladder, he stumbles — apples spill
from the heaped peck basket
and thud soft down. He stoops to them:
perfect galas, heavy and blush dappled,
nestled in the folded golden billows
of grass. They're for the cider bin,
though they seem undamaged. Time,
that healer, will see the bruises blossom
and such a softness
spreads. Not as contagion,
but the way an ache sets in,
or a word.

Silence has a wholeness
that's like a drop
of water. It's called
surface tension. It's called
skin. Once it breaks how words
would pour —

— but he doesn't break. Apples
neat as grenades. He slips one
to swing his pocket: warm and heavy.
flecked with grass, burnt crown tangled with seed.

WINDFALL

In an old habit, Vivian strokes his hair
into sleep. He feels again her hand
growing heavier, her body,
warm and soft and heavy.
Her hand moves and lights
and moves again as she sinks
into sleep. The girls are grown, now.
A fall wind noses through the house
like a dog settling down.
Through the night he hears
the tree stir and rustle
outside the window,
and the apples fall:

One, a breath,
                        then two together.
One.
        Another.

        Another.

LINGER

One morning he woke and found
her body cooling. He tried to lift her
but she was heavy — and that was wrong:
surely there was less here, surely
what he'd lost was solid
as furniture.
                    The coroner came,
the girls and their husbands.
Someone made the bed.
The chenille like snowfall
softened the hollow curve
she'd left. *Slipped away,*
the coroner said, and that was all
he caught. He thought
of how she would let go his hand,
lingering: lifting their arms
between them, her thumb lifting,
her palm's curve rising to his fingertips,
her fingertips brushing his fingertips,
the first inch of her absence
so delicate
                    he hardly noticed.

PASSAGE

Dead, she calls from the edge
of dream. *Where are you going,* he hears.
He's falling asleep and answers: *Sleep.*
How I want to be with you.
As if sleep were her country now,
or as if he had been sent
into the world and now dreamed
to leave it. She was always sad
when he travelled, and lingered at the door.

Over the white highway,
fine snow moves in spirals.
In a blue field, he sees a buck
lift up his head, then arc
into the air, like a bridge of silence.

EMPTY PAGE

SHE COMES TO MEET HIM
Omaha, Nebraska — April 1996

Most of a leg left on a hospital ship —
the rock, the reek of ether.
He learned to walk, after,
but now he's going back
to bone, listing
into old damage.
We meet in the parlour.
He sits and sets his cane to picket
beside him, takes
my ungloved hand.
The young researcher, he says —
a charity. It might be
the young lady, in a yellow dress,
a perfume called Forest Lily,
as if it were a different April
and I had come to see him
carried from the train.
                              Outside,
on Farnam Street, the tulips blown,
the rain.

SNAPSHOT: TROOP TRANSPORT

He's spent the morning below-decks,
practising to break a gun down blindfold —

which never did come handy —

                    but now,
he's leaning on the bow rail,
him and Gawosky, who buys it early,
hamming for someone with a camera —

Who? I don't remember —

turning in that moment into flash
and silver, into paper soft
as Bible covers. Bright-edged,
dapper. A decent boy.

SPARED

Seeing him shaking,
a wordless medic gave him once
a wool cap,
hand-knit,
helmet-matted,
another man's heat
still in it.

He fingers an ear
as if he still feels it,
says
      luck
      close thing
says
      spared

and stops
as if it scares him.

NO DOG

Artillery flashes
far off, sudden blue
in stark heaped pines —

Close up
    no dog would stand for it

On a high bracket
the fan turns its blunt head.
The puzzle spreads between us.

    the noise
he says
    no dog

He snaps together
two pieces of sky.

CARDS

Head dipped, he confesses
the memory of a certain deck

pin-ups. French, you know

French is a code I only half
understand. Impossible to ask
pinups or _____

52 women, and
Paris desperate
as an October rose.
Was he faithful? Vivian
must have wondered

how much of his body
lay spread
on the nubby chenille.

On the wall
the Virgin's pierced heart
pasteboard lifting from its backing —

PLACE

He fumbles a snapshot
from its black corners:
him and Sully hip-deep
in mottled snow.
There's another man with them,
rifle unslung, grey face turning
to a smudge of fire

     can't place him
he says
       And turns
the picture over, cautious,
as if the lost name

were a place,
and one that might take him:
an open field,
a hollow bone,
an empty page.

METASTASIS

The tumour like a hive
sends out its queens,
copies itself in limbs
and hollows.
          Hotspot,
the pain is called:
a press, a match.

No, he says, *a little fist,*
a beat and clench. A voice.

Here at last is a woman's pain,
a pain of additions.

He swells. His spare face
softens.

NATIVE COUNTRY

From Kansas,
slowly,
he learned
silence

The grass comes up
through last year's grass

At noon
hills cast
no shadows

Deer bones yellow
no stink of rot

It became,
again,
his
native country

CUT

From wheat
he learned
to cut
and cut
and plant
again

evening bales
spread out
their capes
of shadow

New grass
comes up
in high summer —
like velvet —

   green fire

THE DEEP

We used to know this:
every opening is a door
for ghosts. Even a yawn's
not innocent. A wound
breaks the body's gates
open. What enters?
Weather wisdom. Phantom
voices. Sadness. Gentleness.
The smell of apples.

Why do they say a leg
is lost? We know
what happened.

       A ship burial:
the splash, the kiss
of salt, the pale light
going slowly out,
the weighted canvas
blossoming open, amputated
legs and hands rocking free —

soft green lights
in the deep
and changing sea.

THE STORY OF GHOST MAPS

Back in 1996, I was researching a novel set during the winter fighting in World War Two's Battle of the Bulge. I needed to understand the endless details of the care of the body, which are most of our lives. The history books gave these short shrift.

The local veterans' group helped me locate a veteran who agreed to talk to me. He didn't want to talk about what had happened to him, specifically. We were supposed to stick to catching sleep in a foxhole, or keeping your socks dry in combat.

Neither of us had understood how intimate the commonplace can be. From the details common to any infantryman, the fragments of his own story began to surface. I saw him every week or so, for about six months. When he died, he left me his combat infantry badge. He never saw these poems.

Carl Hruska was not his name. He asked me not to use his name. The voice in italics, here, is not his voice. But it's not mine, either. It's real enough to let this story be told, and fiction enough to let me tell it.

I changed all of the names, and a few other identifying facts. I imagined some details. But on the whole, I tried to keep true to stories given to me, even when – as with Cologne, or the shipboard amputation – they seem improbable.

These poems are for my friend, and his family, with all my thanks and love.

Erin Noteboom

THANKS TO

The Sage Hill Writing Experience, where these poems were struck by lightning. The poetry workshop there: Betsy Warland, our extraordinary teacher, and my fellow storm chasers Claudia Bickel, Leanne Boschman-Epp, Heather Cullen, Cherie Hanson, and David Miller. The Friends of Anne Szumigalski gave me the scholarship to go.

Gary Smith, this book's first editor, keenest eye east of the Mississippi. Holly F. Pettit, whose WWII book is going to be better than mine. And the rest of the Zeugma online poetry workshop, the perfect combination of generous and snarky.

Claudia Bickel (again), who first showed me the shape of a book in a heap of poems, and believed in this book long before I did.

Maria Jacobs and Noelle Allen at Wolsak and Wynn, who have been passionate — and patient.

My family, including my mom, Rosemarie O'Connor, who cried in the right places; my dad, Wendell Noteboom, who came across the continent to help me celebrate the CBC award; my sister, Wendy Ewell, who completed "Morning" with her beautiful cover; and my mom-in-law Patricia Bow, who was more than the proof-reader.

My husband, my patience, my warmth, my strength, my beauty: James Bow.

ACKNOWLEDGEMENTS

An earlier version of the first four sections of this book won the 2001 CBC Canadian Literary Award for poetry, and appeared in *enRoute* Magazine, February 2002. Some were produced for CBC Radio's *Between the Covers*.

Ten poems appeared in *The Malahat Review*, three in *PRISM international*, and five in *The New Quarterly*, as part of the essay *Different Ghosts: Or Why I Didn't Write an Historical Novel about the Battle of the Bulge*.